Tender

Pitt Poetry Series

Ed Ochester, Editor

Tender

Toi Derricotte

University of Pittsburgh Press

For Cornelius Eady and Sarah Michlem
and the poets of Cave Canem

Published by the University of Pittsburgh Press, Pittsburgh, Pa. 15261
Copyright © 1997, Toi Derricotte
All rights reserved
Manufactured in the United States of America
Printed on acid-free paper
10 9 8 7 6 5 4 3

Derricotte, Toi, 1941–
    Tender / Toi Derricotte.
      p. cm. — (Pitt poetry series)
      ISBN 0-8229-3993-2 (alk. paper). — ISBN 0-8229-5640-3 (pbk. : alk. paper)
      I. Title. II. Series.
PS3554.E73T46 1997
811'.54—dc21   97-4602

A CIP catalog record for this book is available from the British Library.

They were all branded, like sheep, with the owners'
marks, of different forms. These were impressed under
their breasts, or on their arms, and, as the mate informed
me, with perfect indifference, "Queimados pelo ferror
quento,—burnt with red-hot iron."

— Mr. Walsh, "Notices of Brazil" (1860), in Rufus W. Clark,
    The African Slave Trade

He shall feed his flock like a shepherd: he shall gather
the lambs with his arm, and carry them in his bosom, and
shall gently lead those that are with young.

— Isaiah 40:11

Contents

Preface

Tender is not to be read in linear fashion. Rather, it is a seven-spoked wheel, with the poem "Tender" as the hub, each "spoke" or subdivision radiating out from that center.

Violence is central in our lives, a constant and unavoidable reality. Experience is not a linear construct moving from one point to another—childhood to maturity, "bad" to "good," beginning to end—but a wheel turning around a point that shifts between hope and despair.

"At the still point of the turning world," the job of the artist is not to resolve or beautify, but to hold complexities, to see and make clear.

Tender

Tender

The tenderest meat
comes from the houses
where you hear the least

squealing. The secret
is to give a little
wine before killing.

I

Elmina Castle is one of the fortresses in which the slaves were held captive before they were transported across the ocean. Because ships came infrequently and there had to be sufficient numbers of people transported to make a voyage profitable, thousands were often held for months waiting. It is estimated that somewhere between twenty and sixty million Africans were captured, enslaved, and brought to the Americas. The Dutch and Portuguese took slaves from Elmina Castle, a structure built by the Portuguese in 1482, and sent them to Brazil, Surinam, and other colonies. Slaves from Cape Coast, another fortress, were brought to the Caribbean and the United States. Elmina was in operation for more than three centuries.

very historical section → about
slavery and revisiting Africa.

Exits from Elmina Castle:
Cape Coast, Ghana

> Gotta make a way out of no way.
> —traditional black folk saying

The Journey

There is no perfect
past to go back to. Each time I look
into your eyes, I see the long hesitation
of ten thousand years, our mothers' mothers
sitting under the shade trees on boxes, waiting.
There is some great question in your eye that no
longer needs asking: the ball
glistening, wet; the black iris
intense. We know the same things.
What you wait for, I wait for.

The Tour

The castle, always on an
outcrop of indifference;

human shells,
the discards on the way.

Where our mothers were held, we walk now
as tourists, looking for cokes, film, the bathroom.

A few steps beyond the brutalization, we
stand in the sun:
                          This area for tourists only.

Our very presence an ironic
point of interest to our guide.

Tourists' Lunch

On a rise, overlooking
the past, we eat
jolaf with pepper sauce and chicken,
laugh, drink beer, fold our dresses
up under us and bathe thigh-
deep in the weary Atlantic.

Beneath Elmina

connection to the past?

Down the long, stone ramp,
chained together, unchained finally from the dead,
from months of lightlessness and the imprisoned stink
(a foot-square breech,
the cell's only opening for air—air
which had entered sulfurous, having passed over
the stocks of ammunition),
they pressed and fell against each other.
The only other way (besides death) had been for the few
women who were hauled up into the sun
to be scrutinized by the officers,
the chosen pulled up to apartments
through a trap door:
If they got pregnant, they were set free—
their children becoming the bastard
go-betweens who could speak both tongues.

●

At the bottom of the dark stone ramp,
a slit in cement six (?) inches wide,
through which our ancestors were pushed—
the "point of no return,"
so narrow because the Dutch feared
two going together to the anchored ship
might cause rebellion,
and because, starved for so many months,
that opening
was their bodies' fit.

Above Elmina

At the top of the castle,
orderly pews.
We enter under a lintel
carved with news:
This is the house of God.

Slavery

It had struck some of the African Americans
in those dungeons beneath the earth—
though we had come to Africa to heal—there was a huge rip
between us: those were rooms through which *our* ancestors
had passed, while the Africans' had not.
"Another way to look at it," a Nigerian poet answered levelly,
"is that perhaps your ancestors escaped."

Power

The palace of an African king:
two courtyards (a public and a private) in a complex
of bone white stucco edged with a crimson stripe;
the king, in a huge carved chair,
gold-painted and lioned, wearing an understated robe
of grays and browns, his face a structured pleasantness—
the bones of one who has become
slightly more than human;
his ministers smile from faded velvet sofas—
old men with remarkably intact teeth.

A few of us standing in the courtyard
are surprised by a thin man, boyish, though middle-aged,
who comes toward us signaling he is begging—
one hand outstretched, the other nearly touching his lips—
his robe of subtle greens, his feet bare, his naked shoulder
well defined as an aging athlete's. "'The Imbecile Prince,'" our guide explains.
"The only remaining member of the last king's family.
We take care of him as if the present king were his father."

Market

Those huge platters on their heads on which everything
is placed accurately, each small red pepper,
prawn, each orange—arranged in piles so tall they defy gravity—
avocados, crabs, dried fish of silverish brown,
or one great yam, thirty pounds, dirt brushed,
counterbalanced in a kind of aquarium.
A woman approves me with a fluent grin
and offers her light basket for *my* head;
I walk a yard, tottering awkwardly.
The unremarkable commonness—
a beauty shaped by women's hands.

listing

II

When My Father Was Beating Me

I'd hear my mother in the kitchen preparing dinner. I'd hear the spoons hitting the mixing bowl, the clatter of silver falling into the drawer. I'd hear the pot lids clink and rattle. The normality of the sound was startling; it seemed louder than usual, as if she weren't ashamed, as if she were making a point. Perhaps the house was cut in two by a membrane, and, though her *→ poetic* sounds could come to my ears, my screams and cries and whimpers, his demands and humiliations, the sounds of his hands hitting my body, couldn't pierce back the other way. I learned to stretch time and space so I could think what she was thinking. I learned to hear things far away, to live in a thought that could expand itself even until now: What Einstein said is true— everything slows down the farther you get from your mother. *※*

It seemed as if she wanted it, that either I was taking her place, or maybe she thought I deserved it. Maybe there was an overload of violence in the universe, a short in a wire that had to spill its electricity, and she was *→ still poetic* glad, this time, she hadn't felt it.

Maybe there was some arcane connection between her and my father's hand, his arm let loose and flying, maybe she was in command, making him hit, telling her side of the story—that I was evil, that I had to be beaten, not just for the crime I had committed, but for the crime of who I was: hungry, trying, in every way, to get through barriers set up for my own good. "You're tearing me apart, you're driving me crazy," my mother would scream.

Sometimes I saw the world from her perspective: she *was* beautiful and pitiful and overwhelmed, she was also some blood-sucking witch—not a whole being—able to stretch and contort herself like a cry, something that hated and was flexible. She wanted to beat me in the same way my father did, but she knew she couldn't, because I'd fight back, I'd cry that cry that made her go crazy. "You can't manipulate your father the way you can manipulate me." She meant it as a compliment for herself, as if she loved me more.

They wanted a stillness, a lack of person, place, agony swallowed. They wanted me to die, or, not to die, to exist with a terrible pain, but have it sewn up—as if they could reach into my ribs, crack them open, put a handful of suffering in there and stitch it back, as if my body had a pocket, a black pocket they could stick a thought in that they couldn't stand.

Carrying suffering with you

I would fold, collapse like a marionette. (I beat my dolls for years, pounded and pounded and nobody seemed to notice.) "Just keep trying," my father'd say just before he'd strike me. And I did. I kept trying to be beaten.

. . .

Serving the dinner plates with her face bland, as if it were virtuous not to take sides, serving the beautiful food that she had cooked all day—her great gift—to say, *I've given everything I could, I've got nothing left.* Often when my father would hit me she'd say, as if he and I were man and wife, "I'm not going to come between the two of you. You two have to work this out for yourselves." He'd give me a warning. "Wipe that look off your face or I'll knock it off. Dry up," he'd scream, "and eat."

III

Black Boys Play the Classics

The most popular "act" in
Penn Station
is the three black kids in ratty
sneakers & T-shirts playing
two violins and a cello—Brahms.
White men in business suits
have already dug into their pockets
as they pass and they toss in   black v. white
a dollar or two without stopping.
Brown men in work-soiled khakis
stand with their mouths open,
arms crossed on their bellies
as if they themselves have always
wanted to attempt those bars.
One white boy, three, sits
cross-legged in front of his
idols—in ecstasy—
their slick, dark faces,
their thin, wiry arms,
who must begin to look
like angels!
Why does this trembling
pull us?
A: *Beneath the surface we are one.*
B: *Amazing! I did not think that they could speak this tongue.*

↳ Sarcastic

17

sarcastic

Shoe Repair Business

"This shoe is shiny
as a nigger's heel,"
his customer busts out
approvingly. Then, remembering
the shop owner is black, he
tactfully amends, "I mean
shiny as a *Negro's* heel."

Brother

Jay's mother is brown, mine is white-
looking, as I am, as is our father.
He says sometimes when he'd go
to fill the vending machines
with our father, the white bartenders
would say, "Is that your helper?"
My father would say, "No, he's my
son." Jay says you can always tell
the person changes by something
in the eyes, it may be small—
the eyes open wider or the brow
creases down. He says that once,
our father sent him to get something
from the truck. When he came back,
the bartender had set him up
with a soda, "Have some pop,"
he said in a friendly way. Another time,
when I was doing a reading in New Jersey,
Jay was with me. "A yuppie place,"
he remembers. After the applause
I thanked them and said, "I'd like to
introduce my brother." When he stood
up, people were still looking around
for somebody, looking
right through him. finally, when they realized
he was *it,* he heard a woman say, "Oh no!"
as if she had been hit in the solar plexus.
Maybe that's why he didn't marry
somebody like us. He married a girl

19

black as God—and brags to family, strangers,
to *any*one about that
blackness—so easily recognized, his.

Family Secrets

They told my cousin Rowena not to marry
Calvin—she was too young, just eighteen,
& he was too dark too too dark, as if he
had been washed in what we wanted
to wipe off our hands. Besides, he didn't come
from a good family. He said he was going
to be a lawyer, but we didn't quite believe.
The night they eloped to the Gotham Hotel,
the whole house whispered—as if we were ashamed
to tell it to ourselves. My aunt and uncle
rushed down to the Gotham to plead —
we couldn't imagine his hands on her!
Families are conceived in many ways.
The night my cousin Calvin lay
down on her, that idol with its gold skin
broke, & many of the gods we loved
in secret were freed.

Color

21

Has a way of speaking more than writing.

After a Reading at a Black College

Maybe one day we will have
written about this color thing
until we've solved it. Tonight
when I read my poems about
looking white, the audience strains
forward with their whole colored
bodies—a part of each person praying
that my poems will make sense.
Poems do that sometimes—take
the craziness and salvage some
small clear part of the soul,
and that is why, though frightened,
I don't stop the spirit. After,
though some people come
to speak to me, some
seem to step away,
as if I've hurt them once
too often and they have
no forgiveness left. I feel myself
hurry from person to person, begging.
Hold steady, Harriet Tubman whispers,
Don't flop around.
Oh my people,
sometimes you look at me
with such unwillingness—
as I look at *you!*
I keep trying to prove
I am not what I think you think.

kind of like rambling

✳ For Black Women Who Are Afraid

A black woman comes up to me at break in the writing
workshop and reads me her poem, but she says she
can't read it out loud because
there's a woman in a car on her way
to work and her hair is blowing in the breeze
and, since her hair is blowing, the woman must be
white, and she shouldn't write about a white woman
whose hair is blowing, because
maybe the black poets will think she wants to be
that woman and be mad at her and say she hates herself,
and maybe they won't let her explain
that she grew up in a white neighborhood
and it's not her fault, it's just what she sees.
But she has to be so careful. I tell her to write
the poem about being afraid to write,
and we stand for a long time like that,
respecting each other's silence.

weaving two stories together

Passing

A professor invites me to his "Black Lit" class; they're
reading Larson's *Passing*. One of the black
students says, "Sometimes light-skinned blacks
think they can fool other blacks,
but *I* can always tell," looking
right through me.
After I tell them I am black,
I ask the class, "Was I passing
when I was just sitting here,
before I told you?" A white woman
shakes her head desperately, as if
I had deliberately deceived her.
She keeps examining my face,
then turning away
as if she hopes I'll disappear. Why presume
"passing" is based on what I leave out
and not what she fills in?
In one scene in the book, in a restaurant,
she's "passing,"
though no one checked her at the door —
"Hey, you black?"
My father, who looked white,
told me this story: every year
when he'd go to get his driver's license,
the man at the window filling
out the form would ask,
"White or black?" pencil poised, without looking up.
My father wouldn't pass, but he might
use silence to trap a devil.

When he didn't speak, the man
would look up at my father's face.
"What did he write?"
my father quizzed me.

Inventory

In a Charleston, South Carolina, gift store,
the hottest-selling item to this day
is the slave quarters—a little cabin
with a mammy and several pickaninnies.
"We can't keep it in stock!" the saleslady tells me.

Speaking
Narrative

✳ Bookstore

I ask the clerk to show me children's books. I say,
"I'm buying something for my nephew, *Goodnight Moon.*
Are there others you can recommend?" She pulls down
six or seven and I stop her, "Any written by or for black folks?"
She looks as if she doesn't understand. Maybe she has never
heard the words *black folks* before. Maybe she thinks
I'm white and mean it as a put-down. Since I'm white-
looking, I better make it clear. "It's for my brother's son.
'black folks,' black people . . . you know . . . like *me!*"
As quickly as she can, she pulls books from the lower
shelves and loads my arms until the books are falling on the floor.
She wants me to know she's helpful. That her store has so many
to choose from, we couldn't load them in a van. "Thank you, thank you,
that's plenty!" For a moment, history shifts its burden
to *her* shoulders, and the names of the missing are clear.

At a Cocktail Party Honoring
a Noted Old Southern Writer

for Mary Helen Washington

In the middle of the celebration,
she had opened one of the woman's books
at random to that page and, scanning down,

the words had leapt out at her, "We heard
his hoarse nigger voice," that was all.
Amazing, among the thousands of pages,

that she had opened to these words.
The man who had handed her the book
was looking at her, waiting.

Should she point out
the principle distance?
Or would she

take it mildly, not even pointing
to the words as joke. She closed the book
and handed it back. "Out of print,"

he told her, "and one of our great American classics!"
Maybe something had led her
to that very page—

It was *she* who needed to be reminded—
of whom she brings into these places.
She is the actual word!

Workshop on Racism

Her mother is crying
because Briana came home from school screaming in agony.
Two girls in her class are named Briana
and the children distinguish them
by calling her "The Black Briana," taunting her.
She screams at her mother, "I don't want to be
'The Black Briana!'"
Her mother weeps, helplessly. "What can I do?
I give her dolls, read her
black history. How can I protect her?"
Already at five the children understand,
"black" is not a color, it is a
blazing skin.

IV

Invisible Dreams

La poesie vit d'insomnie perpetuelle
—Rene Char

There's a sickness in me. During
the night I wake up & it's brought

a stain into my mouth, as if
an ocean has risen & left back

a stink on the rocks of my teeth.
I stink. My mouth is ugly, human

stink. A color like rust
is in me. I can't get rid of it.

It rises after I
brush my teeth, a taste

like iron. In the
night, left like a dream,

a caustic light
washing over the insides of me.

What to do with my arms? They
coil out of my body

like snakes.
They branch & spit.

I want to shake myself
until they fall like withered

roots; until
they bend the right way—

until I fit in them,
or they in me.

I have to lay them down as
carefully as an old wedding dress,

I have to fold them
like the arms of someone dead.

The house is quiet; all
night I struggle. All

because of my arms,
which have no peace!

      •

I'm a martyr, a girl who's been dead
two thousand years. I turn

on my left side, like one comfortable
after a long, hard death.

The angels look down
tenderly. "She's sleeping," they say

& pass me by. But
all night, I am passing

in & out of my body
on my naked feet.

I'm awake when I'm sleeping & I'm
sleeping when I'm awake, & no one

knows, not even me, for my eyes
are closed to myself.

I think I am thinking I see
a man beside me, & he thinks

in his sleep that I'm awake
writing. I hear a pen scratch

a paper. There is some idea
I think is clever: I want to

capture myself in a book.

I have to make a
place for my body in

my body. I'm like a
dog pawing a blanket

on the floor. I have to
turn & twist myself

like a rag until I
can smell myself in myself.

I'm sweating; the water is
pouring out of me

like silver. I put my head
in the crook of my arm

like a brilliant moon.

•

The bones of my left foot
are too heavy on the bones

of my right. They
lie still for a little while,

sleeping, but soon they
bruise each other like

angry twins. Then
the bones of my right foot

command the bones of my left
to climb down.

Two Poems

Peripheral

Maybe it's a bat's wings
at the corner of your eye, right
where the eyeball swivels
into its pocket. But when
the brown of your eye turns
where you thought the white saw,
there's only air and gold light,
reality—as your mother defined it—
milk/no milk. Not for years
did you learn the word "longing,"
and only then did you see the bat—
just the fringe of its wings
beating, its back in a heavy
black cloak.

Bird

The secret is
not to be afraid, to
pour the salt, letting your wrist
be free—there is almost
never too much; it sits on top of the skin like a
little crystal casket. Under it the bird might
imagine another life, one in which it is grateful
for pleasing, can smell
itself cooking—the taste
of carrots, onions, potatoes stewed
in its own juice—and forget
the dreams of blood
coursing out of its throat like a river.

1:30 A.M.

She can't sleep.
Is she unhappy? Depressed?
Does she need a pill? Is it
her nature? Bottom line: to endure
& write. No pills, no end to
therapy
in sight.
Is there a woman in there
who can't speak?

———————————

It's herself
she can't stand.
She's her own worst enemy.
That's obvious.
Without herself she'd be much better off,
happy, successful,
able to take what she wanted, at least, ask,
good things would mean
something,
be a stepping stone.
"You start & build & tear it all down,"
a fortune-teller says.

———————————

She was miserable.
She left her husband.
She's still miserable.
Did she do the wrong thing?

Was her old misery just an illusion of
her new one, or vice versa?
Perhaps, eventually, if she had stuck it out,
she would have opened like a saint, gained true
cheerfulness, the kind that makes old people's
faces gleam, & be grateful for each little gift.
How can you tell whether, ever, to go forward or
remain? trapped?
bearing what won't abate?
What the Buddhists call
"The Wisdom of no escape,"
the Christians call
hell.

She meditates.

———————————————————

Her father owned a dog that used to hate
him. Whenever the dog would come up from the basement
he'd paw at the door
to go back down. He'd lie down by her father's recliner as if he were
trying to make him happy,
to show him, really, you aren't so bad.
Finally, he couldn't
take his own desire,
he'd start shifting, lifting
up, he'd whine like a dog
who has to pee.
He just wanted
to go back down there by himself
where it was cool & dark, the way someone

with a terrible headache will want to be
left alone, with a cool rag on her head.
Once, to get away, he jumped through the glass door in the kitchen.
Her father told the story as if he were bragging—
that something near him could be that afraid!

You'll never get better.
That thought keeps recurring.
You could get worse. A lot worse.
Some poet leapt off of a bridge.
You wouldn't do that.
You would check into the nearest hospital,
like a cheap hotel you could
always get a room in,
if you discovered a huge roach in your bed.

Where's the victory?
Where's the meat?
A friend comes to the Village in 1970 & falls in love with a
hot dog.
Nathan's The All Beef Hot Dog
the sign says;
ten years later he comes back & notices
a change
Nathan's The All Meat Hot Dog
and ten years later, another change,
Nathan's The All *American* Hot Dog
Memory fades, a few good
jokes remain.

Sex?
Catalogs may be necessary,
like those seeds that come from
faraway places that produce
the best flowers.
Dildos of all different colors!
The mailman lugs their weight
knowledgeably,
in spite of their euphemistic names,
"Open Places,"
he knows the score. For a logo,
there's a woman from a Picasso painting
with a satisfied grin & her hand on her belly.
Mona Lisa wore that look
a woman of a certain age would know.
A woman who knows how to please herself
is gentle,
is her own best lover.

The man in the bookstore on Craig asks,
"Where have you been for the last eight years."
You didn't think he knew your name.
"Buried," you answer.

Maybe you were like those locusts, red-eyed,
eating.
"Your shoulders used to be boxy,
as if you were always trying.
You're milder now," an old friend explains.

VI

Dead Baby Speaks

i am taking in   taking in
like a lump of a dead baby
on the floor   mama kicks me
i don't feel anything

.   i am taking in   taking in
i am reading newspapers
i am seeing films
i am reading poetry
i am listening to psychiatrists, friends
someone knows the way
someone will be my mother
& tell me what to think

---

the dead baby wants to scream
the dead baby wants to drink warm milk
the dead baby wants to speak to her mother
i can't always say the right thing
sometimes i've got to say what feels best
i'm not perfect
but i will not be a lump on the floor
the dead baby wants to kick her mother
the dead baby wants her mother to lie down & let herself be kicked
why not   she let father do it

---

how to separate
me from the dead baby
my mother from me
my mother from the dead baby

nothing is expected
nothing is expected
of you
you don't have to do this or say that
nothing is known
just be   be who you are
a little defiance   a little defense
say, if you want
i lifted up a little

there is that stunned moment when she shuts up & lets me speak
i have nothing to say

then i say
rotten mother who opened your legs
like iron gates & forced me into this prison
who lay among lilies & pressed me to your breasts, saying i will never be alone
        again
who wanted my soul for company, used my body in the place of your soul
who brought me up to the surface by straining off the rich dark broth
until what remained was as vaporous as the shadow of a shadow
whose breasts were bruised fruits

whose legs were swollen tree trunks, but when you were shaken, only one red apple
      fell
whose genitals hold me tethered, a string like a primate's tail, so that i am your
            monkey in the red hat, you are my organ grinder

if you say do not write about me
i will write more
there are many more mouths to feed
than yours
my life is juice pouring
out of me
let it find a channel

i could knuckle under & be good
i could pray for her & turn the other cheek
i could live in her house with her sickness like a stinking body in the stairwell
i could bake bread until my hands puff off
i could sweep the floor
i could suck misery out of my teeth like stringy meat
i could poison her with a plate of sorrow
i could leave the door open on her corpse so that no breath would warm her back to
      resurrection
i could throw myself at her feet
i could languish like a whore in colored rags
i could lie as still as a still life
i could be cut up & served on her table
i could go to my father & beg for her life
i could dance the seven veils while she escapes
i could give to the poor
i could close my legs like a hardened corpse

i could grow into a hag & compare myself to her pictures
i could eat her while she's sleeping
i could put her in the oven & burn her into a lace cookie
i could roar like a gored dragon
i could come crawling like a sexless husband
i could beg her to touch that scratch between my legs which should open in a flower

every time i question myself, i say
mother did not believe me
she thought i was making up my life to torture her
i take off the layers of pain for her to see the teeth marks in my soul
she thinks i can be born fresh once my rotten desires are removed

the desire to touch
the desire to speak

i could clean house until it is empty
i could put everything in the right place
but what about the one mistake i always make

i could love her
i could love her every time she is mistreated
i could love her every time someone forgets to pick up a plate from the table
i could love her weeping in church with a light on her face
i could love her stinking of Ben Gay on the cot waiting for my father to come
i could love her roaming from room to room in the dark with a blanket on, trying to
        be quiet
i could love her eating at night, hungrily, slowly, going back for seconds
i could love her white breasts

i could love her belly of scars
i could love her insides which are half of a woman's
i could love her with the dead baby in her
i could love her though the dead baby could be me
i could love her even if she wants some part of me dead
some part that invades her with sorrow she never understands

---

for the mystery of her childhood
for being too white & too black
for being robbed of a father
for wearing the cast-off clothes of the rich
for eating figs & cream on silver that wasn't hers
for putting the comb & brush neatly in place because they were the only things she
       owned
for learning to make up lies & make everything pretty
(she never believed her own body)
i could love her ocean black hair
i could love it in a braid like a long black chain
i could love her kneeling over the tub cleaning the scum out with a rag
i could love her trying to hit the flying roach with a shoe
i could love her standing in the doorway, thinking she's made the wrong choice

as frail as i
as strange to herself as i
as beautiful as i
as ugly as i

i could do all these things & never be happy

---

worse was done to me she said & *i never told*
i always told
in the body out the mouth
everything from insults to penises
needed words to make it real
be still   you make me suffer
i thought it was i who would die
i thought silence was a blessing
& i was its saint
i was prepared for
a higher calling

―――――――――――――

we are fighting for my silver soul
like Jacob & the angel
you are the angel
i am the young boy fighting for my life
i am the angel
you are the young boy fighting for your life
we mirror each other
like a beautiful face in the river
half of us is drowned
half of us is light
i reach into your soul & pull out the bone of my life

―――――――――――――

my mother is on my mouth
like a frog
be good be good
she points her finger, that old spinster teacher
she points her stick at my tongue

she knocks some sense into it across its red knuckle
half of my tongue hangs like a limp dick
a flag of my mother's country
half rises like a bridge
words might leap across that great divide, a daredevil driver
but i am the driver
& my mother is peeping out of the back like a baby
her eyes big & black with fear

my mother is on my mouth
like a gold frog
she is sparkling & quick as sin
with terrible humped breasts
that nothing can suck at
the black spots on her are universes you could walk on
if she were flat & sound as a board
i take her on my tongue like a lozenge
& roll her around
then i bite down

VII

The Body Awakening

Each morning when I get up I sit with the body.
The clitoris feels dead, hiding;
in my abdomen the tightened muscles
are at cross purposes. Whatever is not felt
in the clitoris is deflected, blocked
in the body like stanched blood. I know the center
of creativity must come
from that tender bud, so circumscribed.
A few weeks ago, at a writer's conference,
my whole body hurt with feelings,
the clitoris throbbed,
I was extruded out of myself,
but when I left that place, came back to my "safe" husband—
the man who loves me and will stay with me
no matter what—I began to feel sheltered,
separated from the most powerful feelings,
and the clitoris too drew back.

·

I question my marriage.
I married my husband because he was a harbor, a safe place
in which I could *stop* feeling.
                        —*What is more punished*
among the angry than anger? among the unsatisfied than desire?
        among the hate-filled
than hate? among the frightened than fear?—
I wanted to be still.

·

Such a ringing clearness, such a transparency
of soul, that most vulnerable & singing part.

*

The clitoris, like the shyest
girl, must not be approached directly, but
as if being entreated to make herself
known, as if being sung to
on a balcony by one filled with love & desire. It is
the buried, deepest secret that must
be loved. Now instead of
demanding that my body respond, terrified
& angry if it doesn't, I
talk to myself, "Relax,
you don't have to
do anything. I won't push or demand."
A determination lets go,
some wall of
protection, skin, the hood around the clitoris,
some psychic box
recedes. I'm with myself, like
being in the presence of one you deeply love.

*

I found the G-spot, its rubbery
quarter of a dime behind the cervix.
I touched it in squat position until I felt its
blood thickening, its full leaf like the thick petal
of the pocketbook plant. This is the place
that makes me feel
as if my womb breaks open, flowers; the pillow

the penis rests on.
A lesbian friend says, a hand is good enough for me.

·

From this I learn
tenderness: I
who have been so demanding
of others—that they show
or prove . . .

We survive on a thin balance,
testing the universe
for signs of love:
As yesterday, gardening, a brown unburied seed, speckled
with dirt & carved with its own particular face.

I found the clitoris, that earthy bulb.
I rubbed myself along the roughened texture of a sheet.
I found the nerves at the small finger's length in the anus.
I have to take myself tenderly
in my hands, listen.
I have to let myself happen, hoping but not certain.

·

A part lets go. I will not
force others as I will not force myself.
I learned to respond in fear—
I stayed
alive in fear. I
beat a life out of myself, a life in which I
made myself smile,

charm, act loving.
I did this by thinking about the possible loss
under everything I did,
thinking that I had already lost everything, lost
my life.

*

Once a great poet said to me: one day
you'll stop sitting there smelling sweet.

*

Those indications are
not to be gotten rid of, every
cinch in my breathing, every awareness of the rivers of
nerve is a song of my self.
My body is instructor,
aching,
or so laid-back
that I feel dead
to myself: To hold all these parts
in consciousness (as if it were
a small thing!), my life.

*

I think with great love of that little hidden seat
of power & wisdom, the clitoris, how it can't be seen
unless (like the face) you look at it with a mirror.

*

This tenderness does not make the
world easy. It

*

is another way to envision living with myself as
the child of a vicious father, & that part always with me.
The old enemy, my aim & direction.
To live with myself; to regulate the unseen
past:
Nothing on earth will change. But this.

For Sharan Strange, After a Reading

Wasn't it your
face I

saw (beautiful!) on
Egyptian

coins, before I knew
those faces

were African? Beauty
only became

yours years
later, coming

into yourself like some
girl whose identity might have been kept

secret
from herself, broken

like the broad nose
of a sculpture.

It's your face—even
with what's been left

out of
history, before and after the naming

of what is so
necessary: It stands

behind you
luminously now.

For Sister Sue Ellen and Her Special Messenger

I thought you were without genitals, that nothing cracked you open and
              made you insatiable.
I thought the blood ran clear out of you like out of the side of Christ—
your body chalk dust, flaking ash,
burning in a yellow godlight;
your brain a seamless garment buried beneath your eyes.

Maybe it was God who taught you cruelty:
the black boy you made sit in his shit until it dried
had to stand up and say *pardon me sister pardon me class*
for the rest of eternity.

You could make a child stutter at her book.
You could make a child recognize his rot.
Perhaps you did it by ignoring, by letting be what had already happened.
A girl carried your words on paper.
Walking down the long corridor under huge stone statues,

what was she but a poor Irish factory worker's daughter
disappearing inside
the harrowing cleanliness and bright light?

At Wintergreen:
A Retreat for African-American Women Writers

One recovering, with the scars down her back where her spine was
        straightened,
scars on both hips, as if
her flesh has been laced back
like flaps or
the wings of a butterfly—
a woman rubs her with oils,
back and shoulders, as if to rub away
some invisible iron cape.
When I started to feel myself again inside of my
body, it was on
and off, like flashes of black light. I had no idea where I went
between, maybe up
looking down through a small, narrow window:
my body with its huge legs like
the freakish legs of some huge bug,
my swimming arms.
Once, with the therapist, I felt something in me, reaching,
a tendril of hope,
and I remembered how,
when my father beat me,
when I'd be lying on the floor, begging,
it was as if a fragile tendril
reached out of my heart, that he might see:
I was his daughter, his flesh, feeling.
I looked up at my therapist and felt for the first time
since childhood
that trembling

even more dangerous
than fear.

The Origins of the Artist:
Natalie Cole

My father
was black, black

as suede,
black as the ace

of spades, black
as the grave. Black

humbled him
and made him

proud. At first
there was a space

between us,
a mirror flashed

back at me. Then
his blackness

entered
me like God.

On Katchimac Bay: Homer, Alaska

I will never forget Diane at the wheel
of that wicked skiff eating
the bay, her intense blue
eyes like the inside of some
ripped-open mountain, how she tended
to us by throwing down
the plastic windows, for the fractures of
ice were flying back in our
faces. We were
down in the middle
of all that, as if our faces had been
pushed down in it, humiliated, as if we were barely staying afloat
on the light of our souls. Something glistened between
us & the water, & then we were
down, down, as much as we were
part of our mother. Icy
breath shook us, like being
born in terror, & the waves
shuddered like some woman
eager to be pleased.

Coming

Molly Peacock in the *Paris
Review* makes me come

back to coming—the poem
about whether she is faking

it, and whether he really
likes it with his head

between her thighs. That wonder,
and wondering

if it is right
to wonder

if he is
the one, the prince of your

second coming, or if you too are just
stuck there, his tongue

on your clitoris like a block
of dry ice. Oh

silver skin
of wondering! that bad

taste in your mouth. The prince may be no more
than an ordinary

husband, the evolution
of repressed

desire wearing
a gold ring.

"What is
love," I ask

a buddy over
lunch, a survivor

of marriage
for forty years. "Well,"

she waffles, "it
depends . . ."

From a Letter: About Snow

for Chana Bloch

I am at a retreat house,
and the nun who runs the house told me to look at my face in the mirror.
I did, but the only thing I keep seeing is the face of Snow, the huge Pyrenees
        sheep dog.
He's so frightened, they can't let him off his leash!
His human eyes, long-suffering, like a saint who's forgotten how to smile.
I hear the breed is naturally shy, and this one was abused by his previous owner.
No wonder he backs away!
But to see a creature so large—120 pounds—so timid.
Once, they say, scared by a deer, he broke his leash and ran.
A mile away a woman stopped with her pickup and he jumped right in!
Who knows why the frightened make decisions!
Today I jogged with him, his thick rangy self leading the way.
Now we're sitting in the shade by the community house while I write this letter.

Death at Still Point

The hunter must be good, because the
prey only screams for a few seconds, as if
it has been startled in its bed and just wants to
protest going. "How can you
do this to me?" it seems to be saying. Its cry
is so brief I wonder if it is still
alive, perhaps hypnotized,
filled with the rapid endorphins.
So often the dying, in the
end, are ready, the way
Alice, after months
of fighting the cancer eating her hips and back, no longer cursed
God, who had been her best
friend, and to the great relief of her friends and family,
her faith returned.
                    At first I
hear nothing—then,
the long silence of the newly dead.

The Blessing

Dear Sister Sylvia,

   You told me I should write a letter to my father, to put all of the anger from my childhood in it. You said I should be totally free and, after, burn it and write a blessing. When I approached you and told you I was having a hard time writing a poem, you clarified, "I don't want you to write a poem. Write a letter, completely free, say what you want, 'Fuck you, you're a shit.' Let go!" I went back to my room realizing I am afraid to let go of "poetry." My writing has been a safe space. I have a boundary around me like that iron belt I feel around my heart when I meditate. When I write a poem I am not just worthless me speaking. I am worthless me speaking as a poet. I am afraid to give up that protection.

   I wrote the letter. Not a great letter, I suppose. After, as you told me, I had to burn it. But where do you burn a letter safely? What if a piece escaped? What if someone saw? What would I say? Would the person think I was irresponsible and dangerous? I decided to go a distance from the new community house in the open field beside the garden. The ground was cold, dampish. Maybe it held some of the rain from a few days ago. I lit the pages and they burned slowly, not flaming, but crumbling like a cigar. I watched it turning into ash, the little flakes on the outside crumbling first. And, suddenly, just when the last pieces of the letter ignited, hail started to fall. Hail. Though there had been no indication, though the leaves were still on the trees. Little balls of hail were falling. I had been afraid that the fire would burn something down and thought, hail could put it out—though there really wasn't that much hail, not enough to put a fire out. And I thought, maybe this is my father's way of reassuring me that my anger won't cause destruction.

   I went into the community house and got several teakettles of water, even though the ashes were cold, and poured teakettle after teakettle on the spot. (I kept coming out every couple of hours till dark just to make sure.) Then I thought I'd do a little dance of celebration. So I went behind the community house where I thought no one would see me, and I put my arms out and did a little Sufi dancing, turning and turning. I hadn't spun like that since I was a child. The world kept swimming and dipping, so that I had to hold on to the side of the stairs until it calmed down. All at once the sky, which had been one long gray sheet, opened, and the eye of the sun, yellow and hot, slid into the crack and shined on me. I said, joking, and out of fear, "God, don't waste your miracles on me!" And, immediately, the sun went back. I felt stunned, frightened, hopeful, but all the old defenses, the iron case around my heart, fell into place.

I reached down to pick up a grain or two of the hail. They didn't melt when I crushed them, but kind of smudged. They were made not only of water, but of dirt, minerals, salt. It was as if the salts out of my father's bones had risen and rained down on me as a blessing

You said that, after I burned the letter, after my rage was gone, when I went to bed, I should see my father and say, "I love and forgive you, Father. Forgive me. Lord Jesus have mercy." In this way we are free. I am not bound by hatred and neither is he.

Not Forgotten

I love the way the black ants use their dead.
They carry them off like warriors on their steel
backs. They spend hours struggling, lifting,
dragging (it is not grisly as it would be for us,
to carry them back to be eaten),
so that every part will be of service. I think of
my husband at his father's grave—
the grass had closed
over the headstone, and the name had disappeared. He took out
his pocket knife and cut the grass away, he swept it
with his handkerchief to make it clear. "Is this the way
we'll be forgotten?" And he bent down over the grave and wept.

The Touch

In my mind's eye
the men were talking politics. I could see
the stacks of the Fermi atomic plant
looming in gray smoke, a distant evil castle.
A broken highway marked the entrance to the city
like the road Christ crawled to his death on.
That was in my mind's eye.
In the eye of my body
the moisture of your kiss
flowed through me.
That first instant when we love!
I opened the door, and you were there, sitting
in a red silk shirt
at a table in the corner, your hair modestly
loose around your face
as if you had turned,
once more, away from the world.
You didn't want to be seen,
but turned toward me,
half-stood, our hands reached,
loosened to each other's arms,
then I came upon your lips.
I have tasted so few women—
But I kept my mouth there,
and you kept your mouth there. I took in
what made me want to love forever, to be lost
in folds and turns
and follow to the meaning.
You are a woman. I wanted

that gravity of the buttocks,
that pushing up of the lungs,
liquid of all your liquid forms,
with one kiss your liquids washed me.
I am stuck.
One touch of your lips has stunned.

Grace Paley Reading

Finally, the audience gets
restless, & they send me
to hunt for Grace. I find her
backing out of the bathroom, bending
over, wiping up her footprints
as she goes with a little
sheet of toilet paper, explaining,
"In some places, after the lady mops,
the bosses come to check on her.
I just don't want them to think
she didn't do her job."

In the Mountains

My beloved was afraid. There was nothing
to be afraid of. But my beloved would not
come out.

       The mountains were the same, shivering
down their dirt bones. The sky
was the same, cloudless, and of such a
blue intensity.
          In the evening on the sill
there was a long bug that whipped its
body like a lash when my beloved closed
the window. Besides that, there
was nothing.
          There had been a word
that broke off in her like the slow
falling of an avalanche. There had been
a look that held up its hands.

       I tried to comfort her, but my
beloved lay down in the
darkness and turned her head
from me, and she would not speak.

On the Miracle of the Crying Statue:
Before You Begin

What a realization to come
to at the end: that the tears
of the saints don't dry, that they cling
to the cheeks of the Virgin for a thousand years, that even
in the poems you write,
if you look back years
later, the tears are still there, un-
finished.
How sad, just as
you begin to move forward,
to open
the creaking
mouth of the body,
to taste again the same tears.

Clitoris

This time with your mouth on my clitoris, I will not think
he does not like the taste of me. I lift the purplish hood back
from the pale white berry. It stands alone on its thousand branches.
I lift the skin like the layers of taffeta of a lady's skirt.
How shy the clitoris is, like a young girl
who must be coaxed by tenderness.

Acknowledgements

Grateful acknowledgment is made to the following publications, in which some of the poems in this collection originally appeared: *American Poetry Review* ("In the Mountains"); *The American Voice* ("Not Forgotten"); *Callaloo* ("After a Reading at a Black College," "Brother," "Exits From Elmina Castle: Cape Coast, Ghana" and "For Black Women Who Are Afraid"); *Crab Orchard Review* ("Grace Paley Reading"); *The Iowa Review* ("Shoe Repair Business"); *The Ireland Review* ("Clitoris"); *Kenyon Review* ("Clitoris," "Passing," "Quandary," and "Tender"); *The Paris Review* ("Bird") *Parnassus* ("Death at Still Point"); *Ploughshares* ("Dead Baby Speaks" and "Invisible Dreams"); *Prairie Schooner* ("At a Cocktail Party Honoring a Noted Old Southern Writer," "Black Boys Play the Classics," "Bookstore," "Family Secrets," "For Sister Sue Ellen and Her Special Messenger," "From a Letter: About Snow," "Inventory," and "Workshop on Racism").

Born in Detroit, Michigan, Toi Derricotte has published three collections of poetry—*Natural Birth, The Empress of the Death House,* and *Captivity*—and one work of nonfiction, *The Black Notebooks*. Among her many honors and awards, Derricotte is the recipient of two fellowships from the National Endowment for the Arts (1985 and 1990), as well as the recipient of the United Black Artists, USA, Inc., Distinguished Pioneering of the Arts Award (1993), the Lucille Medwick Memorial Award from the Poetry Society of America (1985), a Pushcart Prize (1989), and the Folger Shakespeare Library Poetry Book Award (1990). She is a professor in the English Department at the University of Pittsburgh, and she has taught in the graduate creative writing programs at New York University, George Mason University, and Old Dominion University. She founded with Cornelius Eady in 1996 Cave Canem, a workshop retreat for African-American poets.